REFLECTIONS IN THE TIME OF TRUMPIUS MAXIMUS

REFLECTIONS IN THE TIME OF TRUMPIUS MAXIMUS

A Journal in Poems
AD 2016-2021

Mark Fishbein

atmosphere press

Published by Atmosphere Press

Cover design by Senhor Tocas

atmospherepress.com

Table of Contents

Part One: Years of Disbelief

Part Two: The Daily Trumpius

Part Three: The Year of COVID

Part Four: BLM, Pre-Election Jitters

Part Five: The Election

Part Six: The Aftermath

For the Grandchildren
Jaiden, Katya, Leonix

Author's Note to Self:

The idea of this journal came to me after I wrote a few poems about the political climate in the Fall, 2016. I felt I was on to something interesting. Like so many still in shock, I cannot not say his name, and Trumpius Maximus came about. It seems to fit the times. It seems to fit his hair.

What's certain after a few months of this new administration, the America we know will be pushed to its limits, a time like when Thomas Mann's said, "everything is politics". So I'm devoting this diary to the task of finding a way try to capture the times similar to poems and anthologies from the Anti-War 1960's or WWI.

I feel quite helpless to predict anything. The daily reports are so frightening. With such power in the hands of such an unpredictable president (who of course I refer to as "emperor"), we all might not be here in four years.

I strongly believe there are few readers or fellow poets who support the 45th president, the "pussy grabber." This man has no interest in art, no appreciation or wisdom on any subjects other than corruption, bigotry, and machismo. Yes, I've heard politics and poetry rarely mix, but you have to write what you know, and feel. Right now emotion is rampant. I am still in grief. I'm scared.

How will this end? One thing seems clear, this will very likely not end well. History has a way to get its revenge on those who don't study it, including Fukuyama. He never considered 9/11 in "The End of History" and he surely never could have predicted Trumpius Maximus!

Washington D.C., February 2017

Part One: The Year of Disbelief

"*he was...*of little significance to the broad onward movement of human affairs; he was an interruption...a thing like a bacterium of some pestilence. Even regarded as a pestilence, he was not of supreme rank..." HG Wells, on Napoleon.

Kneeling Satyr Supporting the Figure of the Emperor
Severo Calzetta Da Ravenna c.1500 Bronze
National Gallery, Washington D.C.
Edited

Fukuyama's Folly

In the dark age, everything changed.
Learning and wisdom bound in chains.
People dug for tubers in the ground,
Filthy rodents in disease ridden towns;
Life was cheap and death so near
By poisonous waters and foul-smelling air.

But we had progress, all is refreshed!
Such were the loud incantations said,
That on this wounded planet, in our time,
Were visions of peace and the sublime-
The renaissance of such technology
To break the waves of hated history.
But now all hope becomes rearranged,
As Trumpius Maximus takes the stage.

Life is still cheap, death still near,
We forge another centennial of fear.
Everything is forgotten, and nothing redeemed.
Another dark age descends on the fields.
There is no greater sadness: nothing is real.

November, 2016

The Inauguration of Trumpius Maximus

Flamingoes flew in squadrons over the mall.
Rainbows bloomed from the winter clouds
And decorated the adoring crowds.
The heights of heaven from Tiepolo
Shined with the golden Pegasus.
The ground itself trembled like a drum roll–
Not since Cleopatra dazzled Rome
Has such a spectacle been known.

The emperor set his hand on the holy book
To swear his allegiance to god and truth
Leaving its mark of ashes on the cover–
The day America lost its youth.

January 21, 2017

trump l'oeil of insanity

The year is 2017. Now you see it, now you don't.
What's real is a magician's wand,
a wisp of smoke and mirrors, a drone in the fog,
a pantomime of dead elephants and melting ice;
wild dogs howling with the homeless.
It's a monkey house with "alternate facts"-
Which of us has satisfaction?

Tweety-tweets from the Commander in Chief:
it's a monkey house, scatter round the banana tree,
let's all chew on horseshit and bubblegum.
The money smells like honey scum.
Ice cream falls from clouds, patchouli oils the guns,
urine in the wheat beer, fake kisses on fake lips-
Who among us believes in this?

Let madness feed the wear and tear,
ripping weeds from a lawn of despair;
let the pirate flag of chaos flow,
and head for the swamps of Mar-a-Lago.
Don't look back, you'll have a fit,
turn into a pillar of shit!
It's a monkey house here, a real ordeal-
Who the hell among us knows what's real?

February, 2017

II-18
from Eumolpus: Satire in the Style of Horace

Speak! The robes of power have tilted your reason Trumpius
still you tempt again to prowl the heavens for a deal
the gods to suit your vain and capriciousness
          I speak (for those) of the high council 4

See before you named in golden obelisks
     the people await the oracles
hissing in the voices of snakes (gather to feast?)
the temptress with Asiatic loins and soothsayers
                    it is Trumpius they adore 8

You make alliances with enemies against the gods
               it is rumor of the faithless news
  I will tell the tale as a Cyclops with a third eye
    neither you nor your royal concubines
can stop (?) the tide of treason calls 12

the demons arrive as seas rise to the cliffs
     and you can't deny the oracle buddy-boy 16

March, 2017

Spring Snow, D.C., 2017

April came with a pink partition,
cherry blossoms reflected in the river;
daffodils poked in yellow pinwheels
from the lawns of official embassies.
Sidewalks were coral reefs of orchid
among the elm, oak and tulip trees.
Primary colored birds returned to fountains
and chattered about the politics of migration in
a bursting of brightness and fragrance:
it was the perfection of spring in America.

Suddenly sirens screamed in the air-
news flashed of blizzards across the land;
skies darkened to a panic in the wind,
as white ice blew from all directions
and snow fell in a deluge of revenge,
as pink flowers pulverized to white embers.

You, stranger, on these aged streets and tuileries,
where flourished this abundance of spring,
what forces of tyranny were unleashed
while loud birds screamed in disbelief?

April, 2017

Trumpius Nation

To you America, America lost,
How shall we find the faith
To relight the fire in your heart
And raise our freedom torch?

America is now a place to co-exist,
Keeping the insults to ourselves,
Exchanging graffiti on the tv screen
With opinions of each other's sins.

What allegiances could be so crowned,
Delusional, puerile, unworthy of the blood
That spilled on foreign battlegrounds
For refugees of the flood?

The lighthouse on our shore is dim.
The traffic of hope is stalled within.

June, 2017

The Emperor Dozes Off

one day i'll be dead...
what will it matter?
after all, i'll be dead, right?

i'm doing good.
no better or worse
then those other bums.
so much bullshit in the press…

people love me,
that napoleon
what a palace...
that tomb of his,
huge...

france

they had this great fucking parade...
why don't we have parades?

that's a great idea,
with tanks and missiles a mile long.
the generals will love it...
easy sell...

call the kids...

July, 2017

Tweets from No Kingdom

The children of No Kingdom are seduced,
Their spirits hang in the citadel of limbo;
The elders are shattered by the state of siege--
Edicts go unheard for the whispering fear
In hysterical headlines of the idiotic.

The lies spread daily as the vultures feast.
The mongrel priest hoists the fascist salutes
Tweeting from the bowels of No Kingdom,
While burns our lineage to a poverty of ruins;
We have only learned the sorrow of repentance.

Citizen, our tribe is the genesis of slaves,
Blood brothers from famine and persecution.
It is not enough to build a pillared temple
To hide in a sewer of dampness and worms-
What of us, the scavengers who remain?

August, 2017

collapse

tyranny falls
    on frozen ground
pouring into reservoirs of mud

the ministers speak from the side
    of their tongues

the emperor throws lunatic insults
        with nauseous delight

every hour the rain falls
        cold rain
tyranny from above
      from below

all is on shut down
    on high alert

shattered
diseased
scandale

October, 2017

Populusque Trumpius

Their faces are wrinkled by desert sun.
With bodies fat from cloned potatoes.
They carry firearms to the fireman's ball,
And listen to music which makes you crawl.
Meeting at the neon bar for beers,
Sneering at anyone who doesn't live near.
They're the good souls from the heartland-
Don't presume to be their friend.

They believe dinosaurs roamed in Eden
With a blue-eyed Adam and straw blond Eve;
Still their shamans and holy men rattle
From the podium of the coming battle
Between Jehovah and the tribe of Satan,
For thousands of years and still awaitin'.
They're the good souls from the plains-
Don't presume they hear a word you say.

They have sad smiles with puffy cheeks
From years of grinding their angry teeth
About the type of folk that don't speak their speak.
They use all the tools of technology;
The car drives, the cellphone rings, the ice box cools-
Yet they think all science is for godless fools.
They're the good souls of the main street towns-
Don't presume they want you around.

There's no chorus or parlor dance to share,
There are no poets or dreamers near.
It was once we joined in noble labor
Of building a nation of neighbor to neighbor.
But like owner and slave or peasant and king
They cling to their own, a religious thing...
They're the good souls of America today-
Don't presume they want another way.

January, 2018

Dying Bigly

What operas to be made about Trumpius!
He the mad baritone,
with the fashion-frigid wife, a mezzo-
no Desdemona her!

Will he linger on and on
like Franco or Philip the Fair,
like Fidel or the aging Pharaoh,
exiled like Napoleon,
to become an old gardener
or Khadhafi in the streets
his eyes ripped from their sockets?
Maybe he will find god like Saddam Hussein
in a cage with a vacant gaze?

It's a Satyricon from imperial times,
Eliot's Shakespearean rag:
Le Grand Duke of malevolence,
Reality TV Mephistopheles.

Alas, the final blow
to choke
on a chicken bone?

February, 2018

The Daily Hate

I was taught to hide my hate,
A bully who slaps my bleeding jaw;
I keep it muzzled and on a leash-
Let it scream in the vacant woods.

But Trumpius salts the wound
As he jerks-off on the cellphone
Spreading sour scummy lies
To his media-mob to idolize.

I hate most that I spend days in hate,
The very precious hours I'm awake
Scheming unspeakable assassinations-

Do Yoga. Write a rant. Play Pergolesi.
Breathe in. Breathe out. Breathe in.

March, 2018

Boneheadedness

Antique assholes blow their noses
Reality's in a free for all
There are no doves or bleeding roses

Dignity begins to decompose
The Emperor's tweet has made the call
Antique assholes blow their noses

George Orwell tell politicos
Stop praying to the wailing wall
There are no doves or bleeding roses

Confidants lay in the shadows
Tyranny! shouts from halls
Antique assholes blow their noses

Stupidity is a hidden clone
DNA is Neanderthal
There are no doves or bleeding roses

History will soon foreclose
What was truth before the fall
Antique assholes blow their noses
There are no doves or bleeding roses

April, 2018

i really don't care do u

she is lost to her shopping.
rooms of shoes to be worn once or twice
bored of her sunglasses
she orders new bathrobes today

in desperation the immigrants arrive
babies torn from the mother's breast
screaming in foreigners' arms
o soft spoken beauty
this is your evita moment
to spread your magic fashion smile

beloved queen
shed a tear on your slavic cheek
and wave your wand   all
all will adore you

she chooses a curious graffiti
to wear on her coat
for the photo-op with the children
well behaved in their cages

it was a fashion statement
her handmaidens claim
the last cutie who made merry
said *let them eat cake*
seems she lost her head

but i don't really care do u

May, 2018

Independence Day, 2018

July brings punishing rays of sun.
I sit alone, in the shade of leaves
In a mist of sweat on the National Mall,
Taking refuge from the sweltering
Which brings such sinister times.

Before me a spider, master at his craft,
Oblivious to the seasonal heat
Wraps his prey in a coffin of silk
Paralyzed and buried alive
As I am trapped in a web of lies.

July 4, 2018

Trumpius Trash

We will remember what these people were made of
Those who follow the buffoon to their graves
They will bear no name of honor above.

The pompous parade of adorers' love
Filled with a venom of greed and rage
We will remember what these men were made of.

Those who follow the buffoon to their graves
And praise his name on the public stage
They will bear no name of honor above.

In their mockery of shame to be proud of
They would lock the truth in a cage
We will remember what these men were made of.

In private they curse what they have done
As they add their names to the list of shame.
They will bear no name of honor above.

Faces red from the slap of a glove
Insults to this nation we would save
We will remember what these men were made of
They will bear no name of honor above.

August, 2018

Sentence Examples with the Word "Trump" in the Year 2040

The meat is rancid. It has been left to **trump**.

These mosquitos keep **trumping** my legs!

He smells of **trump.**

Instead of saving the drowning child, he **trumped.**

The wife was **untrumped** when the casket was opened.

The baby was premature and suffered the **trumps.**

She drank too much and **trumped** in the bus.

That fresh mouth will get you **trumped** one day!

He lowered his head at the verdict, then **trumped.**

I've not heard such a pile of **trump** in a while!

Look, you don't **trump** me, I **trump** you!

It was like lying in a bed of **trump.**

If you have a friend so true, **trump** him before
he **trumps** you.

Being made the fool, he prayed to the **trump**.

Say not what can't be **trumped**!

September, 2018

Paradise, Ca.

And where do we go now? Do we go where tides rise and flood the streets, or where tap water catches fire? Do we join the refugees from the coastline battered by storm? Do we go to the swamps filled with yellow slimes, or the shores with cancerous fish? We see our images on the TV screens, those who have lost all. In the horizon our Paradise is black in smoke. Did we so disobey the word going down, we who are cast away like dark angels?

Paradise, Ca.

Paradise burnt down to the ground.
The church is a rubble of scorched stone.
The gravestones are black windows
Where the scattered marble angels lean
In crooked angles in horrible whiteness.

Quickly the Nightly News switches to other scandals and seeks a scapegoat for the blame. Ours was the dream of earthy bliss...

Paradise, Ca.

How well we had chosen our boarders,
Far from the wickedness of winter,
Far from the refugee camps of tents
Filled with victims of war and tsunamis
That is shown on the nightly news;
Far from the immigrant squalor
In the history of their own bloodline.
We came to Paradise, California,
And built our walls to hide behind.

This place was founded with immigrants and poverty, but all the world wanted part of it. We were nestled in the wine country, where folks dressed in floral printed shirts, with handsome horses on the roadside. "Let them find their own paradises," we said. This was ours, each man his own militia, like the book of freedoms says, each family minding their own ways.

Paradise, Ca.

The Emperor speaks of his greatness,
To the cheers of *all for one*
And tweets his tears to the royal vials,
As the earthquakes and fires go on.

The insurance companies find small print,
All offer thoughts and prayers.
The banks say credit is tight.

The citizens of Paradise scatter
To the backstreets of America
Collecting public aid.

"Losers" the Emperor says.

November, 2018

"Make America Great Again"

Empires do not rise again,
only once do they plunder the world
with brutal force from land or sea
to adorn their palaces with luxuries.

Empires do not rise again.
as they stumble they fall, broken, resigned
to being crippled,
building walls and abandoning alliances.

Empires do not rise again.
They do not survive the greedy tumor
from the bankrupt coffers of the state
spreading to the ministers of doom.

The past is worshipped like a golden cow-
things were always better then.
Our empire fell the day he said
"Make America Great Again".

December, 2018

Notes: Years of Disbelief

Fukuyama's Folly, November, 2016
Yoshihiro Francis Fukuyama's book, *The End of History and the Last Man* (1992), was a best seller and frequently discussed in the 1990's. He argued that the worldwide spread of liberal democracies and free-market capitalism of the West and its lifestyle would signal the end point of humanity's sociocultural evolution and become the final form of human government.

The Inauguration of Trumpius Maximus, January 21, 2017
In a press conference, Sean Spicer, Trump's White House press secretary, stated that the crowd "was the largest audience ever to witness an inauguration, period, both in person and around the globe", and accused the media of reporting false crowd estimates to "lessen the enthusiasm of the inauguration". This was contrary to areal photographs of Obama's inauguration.

trump l'oeil of insanity, February, 2017
Kellyanne Conway introduces "Alternate Facts".

II- 18 Satire in the Style of Horace, March, 2017
In this Ode, Eumolpus (1949-c. AD 2047) refers to the period when Trumpius first took the high council. The oracles, printed matter or newspapers and "social media" proved to dislike his mannerisms and wealth. He called these *prophesie falsum nuntium*, literally *"fake news"*. "Buddy-Boy" was chosen for *amicus phaulius,* for the implied satire for which Eumolpus was known for in his later writing. It was impossible to render the Asclepiadean meter from stanza to stanza perfectly into English to preserve the text, especially in the case lines 4, 11 and 16: (/uu/uu/ u/u //u /uu *Translator*).

Spring Snow, D.C., April, 2017
A foreboding snow ruined the Cherry Blossom Festival.

Tweets from No Kingdom, August, 2017
"He shall stretch the line of confusion over it... They shall name it No Kingdom there, and all its princes shall be nothing". Isaiah 34 8:15

i really don't care do u, May, 2018
The first lady wears a jacket with an unusual message that will define her in history. She was visiting immigrant children, refugees on the Southern boarder separated from their parents living in cages.

Independence Day, 2018, July 4, 2018
In Washington D.C., at the National Mall.

Trumpius Trash, August 8, 2018
Dedicatedto the GOP Senators, the family, the whole Trumpius tribe.

Paradise, Ca., November, 2018
Fires erupt in the west, and the town of Paradise burns down.

Part Two: The Daily Trumpius

Graffiti of Nero found on Roman Wall AD 60

Graffiti of Trumpius in Edinburgh, Rebel Bear, AD 2020

"And when you're talking about an atmosphere, oceans are very small. And it blows over and it sails over." Trumpius

The Great Wall Debate

I

Passions ran quite high and went on for months. It was so inane, it questioned the value of education in our civilization.

Pro:
We shall be so proud of the wall!
It will be seen from the space station,
Unlike ancient walls made of stone.
It will be made of steel slats
To look like vertical window blinds
In the homes of the rich and famous.
Those remnants of the Inca and Aztec,
Let'em bury their corn infested bodies
In their jungles and leave us be!

Con:
Graffiti will be sprayed
With the quotations of Chairman Xi,
Malcom X and Jay Z.
It will confuse the migration of jaguars.
We shall be hated for our wall.
As the Pope says, "Walls are immoral."

Pro:
Ali Baba, Poncho Villas, thieves be thwarted;
There's no telling the difference
Between a Mexican and a Taliban,
Drugs and rapin', 24/7.
Comin' here for Medicare
Just for cleanin' toilets and picking peaches-
Fuck'em! Build the wall
And let 'em pay for it all!

Con:
What happened to give me your tired your poor?
Who will play shortstop for the local team?

Who will watch the children
when you go to movies?
Who will come to clean your asshole
when you're old and mean?

II The Government "Shuts Down"

Trumpius fires the knights from the table
And demands completion of his medieval moat.
Museums, parks and shrines close their doors,
Even tax collectors go without pay.

He tells the unemployed to shovel shit, or babysit,
And tweets "I take full responsibility"
Adding "but blame the bumbling senators,"
Claiming his wall extends a thousand miles.

At the great academies of learning is a chorus
Of indignation, the rest of us with a vague nausea,
Heads slumped within our shoulders, watching videos
Of empty desert, wondering what the fuck America is.

January, 2019

Daily News

Headlines doggie paddle down the stream
Merrily merrily   all's a dream

Earthquakes   tsunamis   tornados   typhoons
Children starving   Suicide bombings
A bengal tiger escapes from the zoo
Trumpius tweets it's all fake news

Shithole countries suffer drought
Harry the chimp diagnosed with gout
Hummingbirds die in record amount
Trumpius hides his bank accounts

Marijuana to increase sperm count
Fashion update   eyeglasses go round
Seas to rise above the ground
Trumpius to fit a golden crown

***

My brain in a bubble bath
Fake fairy tales   fake views

Freedom is fake   fake is news
A thing with nothing left to lose

February, 2019

The Weekly Rally

Pickup trucks with chrome faces
Fill the arena parking lot.
Thousands wave with printed signs,
Shouting t-shirt slogans:

down with the deep state
down with the media
keep the damn government out
of my Medicare

The Emperor enters, waving with glee.
"Trump-i-us!" they salute
As he hugs the flag like a pin-up girl
And leads the chant of "lock her up",
(Though none remember what she did or why),
And then spits and spews conspiracies
Of those who suck the teat of the state,
The socialists who practice infanticide,
The invasion of the brown barbarians
In a run on sentence for hours!

At last he concludes with statesman-like flare
" It's all bullshit my friends" to a fanfare
Of adoring faces, with that sadistic nuance
That drunk men understand who curse their lives-
"Yeah, all bullshit!" they resound,
"Let him burn the system to the ground!"

At last he waves goodnight
Making silly faces of a vaudeville clown.
He points his middle finger at the cameras
Reminding all that his tales are true,
Or should be.

March, 2019

I am *They*

They are not barons who buy shares in the "deep state."
They are not conspirators, or a filthy soup of anarchy.
They hold to be the arbiters of sacred pledges,
And *They* will not bend a knee to the Emperor-

I am *they!*

Camera smiles, veneers that cover fangs,
Shining white as snow, snake oil salesmen of the good book,
Cry the desecration of the American way,
Before the foreigners came-

I am *they!*

We the people have lost their way;
I will not break bread with their decay.
Trumpius is tax-free in the palatial zone,
Insulting our intelligence from a vulgar throne-

I am *They!*

April, 2019

Grounds to Impeach

My father taught me to tie a tie
As a gentleman will be defined
Like a lady by her hat or scarf.
He was born poor to immigrant stock
But in his prime he'd buy these *objects d'art*
From the best silk printers in Italy
With exquisite colors and design-
In a crowd he sparkled like vintage wine.

Most important is the placement, he'd insist,
In the center of the belt the tip must fall-
So when you sit, sthe fabric doesn't twist
And standing, it doesn't cover your balls...
Retying the knot
Over and over for the perfect spot.

Now, Trumpius wears cheap looking solids
Way below the crotch, it's squalid-
When he sits it hangs like a frock,
And when he stands it wags like a monkey's cock.

It's an embarrassment everywhere
To anyone with fashion flair-
Forget the 10,000 lies, the affairs so crude,
That nagging voice from the ego platitude;

Impeach the son-of-a-bitch goodbye
Who can't even learn to wear a tie.

May, 2019

Vomit Mouth Resigns

Vomit Mouth addressed the press,
Chunks of lies with the stench of bile.
At last some relief! She quits her post.
The pundits count their blessings.

If there is goodness in revenge
As many people would agree,
Vomit Mouth will disappear
From all the TV screens.

May she be jeered by all her neighbors,
Everywhere she goes to feed,
To remind her of the phony speech
When she stuck her forked tongue
Up the asshole of history.

June, 2019

Independence Day, 2019

Children were given chewing gum
and seated in the center stage,
their Shirley Temple faces shine;
Trumpius takes the podium
as they sway side by side.

All went according to design.
Jet fighters and stealth bombers
dove from clouds with eagle grace
to a supersonic thunder.
The Navy Choir accompanied trumpets
as flags raised and fingers curled
in hand-signs of white supremacy;
red faces chanting *U-S-A!*

Then the oratory began-
the conspiracy of diplomacy, the brilliance of his riches,
intoxicated formulas to make America anew
out of schoolyard rules.

Balloons were released from the nets,
red and blue lollipops filled the air,
and the children sang in unison,
raising their arms like spears.

I was passing by on my bike, curious to see.
As a Jew, it was hard to breathe; I was afraid-
I stood up, and silently went my way.

July 4, 2019

Cape May Afternoon

There was a time, I remember,
a resort town like this, in soft August breezes.
There were few who were Black, or Asian.
I was White and privileged, too,
but never thought of it as such.
I was a boy, and my hair was blond as straw.
Was that when America was great?

Today on the ferry I saw a group from India-
the women in bright silk saris made brighter
by their pastel brown complexions,
the men with Sikh beards and tailored tunics.
They sat alone in excluded silence.
They were passed by my fellow citizens,
in loose jeans, t-shirts covering their round bellies,
families and friends sporting MAGA hats.

Waiting was the village center, the marina,
and the fanfare of souvenir shops,
the smell of chocolate fudge
seeming to come from the ocean.
An orchestra played Leroy Anderson
under the bandshell draped in bowtie flags,
the kids in the psychedelic game arcades
shouting with crashing cars and pop-guns.
It was the America we all expected;
the architecture of coastal New England
A mix of Southern and Victorian facades,
airplanes skywriting *Hard Rock Cafe,*
cotton candy, family tandem-bicycle rides.
And so many wore the red hat, like a badge;
all knew the message of outrage they sent.
Everything felt wrong, joyless and sad.

***

They say Trumpius speaks for them;
the voice against the progress of greed,
the social engineers, the atheists,
populations of oily haired immigrants
who suffer with English, their children
flooding schools with eager expectations;
the victims of globalization, fake news,
their neighborhoods open to all.
The parade of faces thirst for sameness-
Can we ever love each other again?

Damn the past! The Civil War, slavery,
racism from the Mayflower and conquistadors,
the prejudice against my people, and yours;
we all were once from a land of sorrows,
our generations struggled for equalities.
But we are here, now, in this summer waltz-
what does history have to do with us?
Can't we join as patriots and friends,
proud that we are, as a nation, the ideal?

We strolled past lawns with full hydrangeas
in lilacs, blues, pinks and whites.
Among us too, so many colors and tongues.
I am not young anymore, nor is my country,
but I remember the welcoming smiles
in a day like today before this reign of hate.
The red hats speak of cold revenge
where sadness rules on streets of change.

August, 2019

The Daily: 9/22/2019

there's a rat crawling in the kitchen
but we return each morning
    for our daily soup
    filled with filth
every day we swallow more

tomorrow we will forget these todays
    he said he could wipe afghanistan away
    he said windmills cause cancer
    he claimed to be chosen by god
        to make trade wars with china
 all this we will forget

 because tomorrow
    he will blame the fish for forest fires
    aliens for stealing the bodies of democrats
    he will say ice cream cures cataracts
    he will declare war on costa rica
 because he has inside information
 the oracles tell him to be transparent

 we will forget today and tomorrow
        and the thousands of sentences that contradict
        and the spectacular self-praise

we will remember
    the flavor and crunch
    of the water bugs
    swimming in the soup
as we returned each day
      for psychotic nourishment
watching a rat pacing in the kitchen

September, 2019

The Mission

The terrorist has blown himself up
Wearing his fucking Rolex watch.

The terrorist with the white and red beard
Sweaty and overweight with red eyes.

The terrorist with the grey robe
Hiding in a tunnel with a suicide vest.

By his side were his young children
With shit in their pants.

The ground absorbed their guts
And fire charred the bones.

Trumpius declares triumphantly
Another victory to praise my name!

O leave us be this Sunday morning.
One enemy is dead, another fills the ranks.

This man who lived for vengeance,
The joy of the kill was gain enough.

Trumpius mocks the death and claims the prize.
The great executioner. None was surprised.

October 28, 2019

chairman dunce

vile vile villainville
    stone faces with stone eyes
        chairman nunes denies denies

gangster chattering
    vile vile villainous bile
        putrid silence from the aisle

killing fields of venomous vile
    spit&fires   vilascious cries
        sewers with stink of lies and lies

scabs of words are specked and dried
    trumpius vilis vilis vile
        vomit chunks of nunes bile

hatred reeks no viler times
    obese the shit of shame to hide
        and vile the ooze of truth

and chairman nunes to the call
    to fill the chamber with his bile
        putrid and so so vile

November, 2019

Maximus No More

Point if disorder.
There is profound disorder in the chamber.

They dueled with words of steel.
Now the ping of silence deadens.

Abuse of Power! Obstruction of Congress!
Trumpius empties his bowels.

Get over it, the spokesmen say,
Like a punishment for bad manners.

The emperor tells the aisle of spies,
Truth is mere conjecture. Deny !*Deny* !

Teeth are ground, eyes stare at eyes.
Order and disorder. The vote arrives.

The jargon of lies fills with fear-
Ashes fall like snowflakes.

Now the hour inequity falters;
Trumpius Maximus is Maximus no more!

The deed is done, but cheer is fading.
On to the Senate where orators snore

And nobles rant like vagrants
Who scrape the gold mines clean.

Point of disbelief! Trumpius in a tiff.
And none allowed to bear witness.

***

There is the seasonal stillness in the halls
All flee with promise of the New Year.
Citizen Trumpius now baptized in shame.
History to drop the Maximus name,
Point of order, point of disorder;
but everybody knows he will remain...

December, 2019

Killing the Bad Guys

A drone *tookout* that bum, Soleimani.
Iran's blood pressure is sky high.

He was planning bad things, what a bad guy!
Everyone agrees and rolls their eyes,
The list of bad guys goes on for a mile.
But for now there'll be no battle cries,
Just more drones to fall from the sky,
And their revenge by suicides.

Trumpius takes the praise in style,
To take-out enemies who would hide,
Finding targets on a shooting range
To make them martyrs in exchange

January 2, 2020

The Acquittal

The white haired senators are solemn,
Trapped in a chamber of silent pomp.
They pledged their souls to Trumpius
And defy their pledge of public trust-

Corruption is the core of our ways
The simple truth since we crawled from caves.
All rise and salute the great tycoon
The alpha male in the hall of baboons.

The time of the tyrant has been restored
Trumpius to rise above the law.
The Senate will not impeach-
He tweets to be *the magnificent.*

February, 2020

Notes: The Daily Trumpius

Grounds to Impeach, May, 2019
Written 8 months before the real impeachment began.

Vomit Mouth Resigns, June, 2019
"Vomit Mouth", so named by a MSNBC contributor, due to blatant lying during live conferences as the Press Secretary in 2019.

Independence Day, July 4, 2019
"...fingers curled/ In hand signs of white supremacy..." This is official hand signal of Supremacists, making the "O.K." gesture.

Cape May Afternoon, July, 2019
Cape May New Jersey is the nation's oldest beach side resort, established 1800.

The Mission, October 28, 2019
Death of Baghdadi, leader of Isis.

Maximus No More, December, 2019
After the passing of the Articles of Impeachment, and no agreement to accept a trial in the Senate, Trumpius is impeached by the House of Representatives.

The Acquittal, February, 2020
In a candid conversation with my next door neighbor, a Republican Senator, I am told what the senators fear most-themselves. The gist of the conversation was we cannot impeach for stupidity, because then every president would spend his entire tenure being impeached. I felt the Senator was truly being honest. Politicians see each other as rotten to the core.

Part Three- The year of COVID

The angel of death striking a door during the plague of Rome;
Engraving by Levasseur after Jules-Elie Delaunay

Panic Fever Armageddon

The staff of fate puts a burden on our lives
Plague upon the land   marketplaces close
Gatherings cancelled   sporting events and travel end
                    Panic   Fever   Armageddon

Trumpius says it will pass   time will conquer through
It's a mere distraction   a case of flu
Don't let hysterical scientists rule
                    Panic   Fever   Armageddon

The elderly are most at risk   perhaps their time has come
But not me   in perfect health   says the surgeon
More fake news from the fake news scum
                    Panic   Fever   Armageddon

The streets of cities are silent and empty
All stare out the window   afraid to breath
It was the Chinese   don't blame me!
                    Panic   Fever   Armageddon

History repeats   the Spanish flu   a hundred years ago
Fear in our eyes like we have never known
The mask of red death at the ball
                    Panic in a fever of Armageddon

March, 2020: Week 1

Daily Briefing Rage

Swarms of vagrants storm the malls
Pitchforks raised for toilet rolls-

The shelves bare, emergency declared.
The gates slam shut; mass graves prepared.

Bad omens loom, all nations cry-
Threats of coughing innocents die!

Trumpius, tell us what the state provides!
Mumbles his polls are high, ad libs fly…

Try hydroxychloroquine,
Brush your teeth with distilled bleach.

Of all his performances throughout these years
This is more than the press corps can bear.

Let the alchemists have their say!
Enough is enough! Get off the stage!

March, 2020: Week 2

A Hunkering Down:

I'm a hunkering down, down, down.
A hunker down ye brethren and maidens
And thou elders, a hunker down!

New on Netflix, going viral,
"A Hunkering Down in the Hamptons".
A hunker down with a cellphone and Pornhub.
Wash your hands. Learn to Zoom.

> The congress of experts disagree:
> hospitals overrun, oxygen in low supply,
> the floor manager decides who lives or dies,
> ambulances search for parking spaces,
> dead are stacked like a fish on ice-
> It's bluntly medieval. Send in the leeches.

So I'm a hunkering down like a mole.
A hunkering down, down, down,
#hunkeringdown.

March, 2020: Week 3

Plague in the time of Marcus Aurelius and Trumpius Maximus

By Marcus Eumolpus, Historian

It is well recorded that 2000 years ago Rome was victim to a plague. Today we believe the Antonine (or Galen) Plague was brought from either China or Iran, and was probably smallpox. It lasted for 20 years, killing 25% of the population, 2,000-5,000 daily in the capital city. People stayed at home, kept social distances, and wore face coverings, as it was believed the disease was passed in the air. The pandemic came in waves. Populations were quarantined. Hysteria and sadness were pervasive.

Marcus Aurelius (AD 121-180) was emperor for most of those years. Aurelius is famous for his "Meditations," a private diary of thoughts and observations which he had requested to be destroyed at his death. Fortunately some of them survived and show him to be highly eloquent, compassionate, wise, and spiritually uplifting. Quotations derived from his scrolls are seen today in government offices, philosophy books, poetry, and yoga studios. Many agree with the evaluations, from Machiavelli to Edward Gibbons, that he was THE greatest ruler in history.

In the 2nd century AD, Rome was at its height. The economy was free and growing in an early form of capitalism. Science, medicine and technology would not be surpassed until the industrial revolution. Accumulating wealth was a good thing. The government was functioning; Aurelius worked closely with the Senate and regional governors during a period of political cooperation. Corruption was not endemic. Roads and sanitation, public buildings and monuments were abundant in the vast territories from current day Scotland to Cambodia. At that same time, a pandemic was spreading around the world with terrifying death. Aurelius inspired Rome to persevere. In AD 178 he even sold off the imperial jewels, which belonged to him as emperor, to put more cash in the plague depleted treasury, rather than add taxes to an already suffering population.

Looking at the world through "big history" there are overwhelming similarities between our nation and the old Roman empire. America can be said to be modeled on Roman law and society. Consider the architecture of our government buildings, and the concept of law and division of state. After all, many "dynasties" can exist within an "empire". As Zhou Enlai said about the lessons to be learned from the French Revolution, "it's too soon to say for sure." To the Chinese, George Washington was just a successful Spartacus.

Historians largely agree that the Antonine Plague was instrumental in eventually weakening the empire. Economically and territorially, it caused an immediate loss of influence. In his time, Aurelius managed to maintain the Roman grip. But after his death the empire fell in the hands of lesser known emperors. As today, the plague stretched the empire to the limits, no more prepared for it than if a meteor hit the earth.

How can we compare our current leader, Trumpius, with Aurelius? It is most curious that they are exact opposites in all considerations. Aurelius had one wife and never remarried after her death. He came from a patrician family, learned Greek and the classics, and served in the Senate for many years before taking, reluctantly, the post of emperor. He was a deep believer in the traditional gods. His diet was based on healthy recipes which he encouraged others to follow. He lived his life with moderation and humility. He also performed his military duties and protected the empire with victories and forged alliances.

Now, let us look at Trumpius. His opus is "The Art of the Deal", a treatise on how to take advantage of people for personal gain. Raised by a common real estate family, he expanded the business with unscrupulous practices and bankruptcies. He is admittedly poorly read and clearly uninterested in philosophy or history. He was married three times, in addition to being notoriously unfaithful. He eats the most unhealthy diet. The number of public lies and made up facts he has said, are in the thousands. He uses the power of his office to openly procure arrangements on his properties. He is the*Anti-Stoic* . Philosophers refer to his *logos* as *Neo-Peter Panism* or *Neo-Pornism.*

J'Accuse!

Trumpius has no plan to control the forces around him. Hundreds of millions now stay at home behind locked doors, as thousands die daily from lack of preparation for a predicated scenario of possible catastrophes (be they flood, famine, or pandemic). He is accused of poor judgments in the early days of the epidemic, allowing it to spread without listening to his advisors. He is enraged by such claims, inventing new falsehoods from one day to the next. He offers shallow clichés of lamentation for the dead and dying in this spring of AD 2020. He only speaks of his greatness. These are historical facts. Unlike 2000 years ago, recording devises now exist.

Yet many of our citizens crave for a "Caesar" to aspire kingship to. It proves again that Plato was right. Democracy will only work when it is not left to the whims of the poorly educated classes. The *populusque* live in resentment and fear of losing their wealth or identity to invading tribes of alien hordes, who slave for them at low wages. They aspire to his contempt and greed. He corrupts with a flow of conspiracies, filling his followers with paranoid slogans. This must end or we will enter the final decline of our Roman traditions: *the media is the message*.

So it is this day recorded
Personal note to future historians on AD April 8, 2020, Eumolpus the Historian has joined the resistance! May the winds of virtue purify us!

April, 2020 Week 4

the mask

he arrives daily to the podium to defend his motley measures
every day for hours and praise his noble wisdoms and lies since
history began since the spoken word since the invention of fire
since we crawled from the slime   no human before has been
right and never wrong trumpius is told to
wear the mask   o should he die we are lost
ministers around him cover their faces and their eyes
with paper towels with napkins with scarves with rubber
bands to wear as gags to muffle the panting and hide their fear
he chooses to without such an ugly thing to greet dictators he
invites to his oval orifices the virus will come he dares it
to a duel not if   but when he will scuff at it and absorb
a chorus in adoration of endless self-pity yes to see
him fevered and panting as a frightened dog but not to die and claim
the headlines of our time first he must break down cry like a baby
plead for forgiveness with his hair undone cursing chinese toilet
paper he uses in his daily dump tweeting his final tweet

April 6, 2020 Week 5

The 2% Deal

A bean bag has 100 beans. Two are poison.
Odds vary. Nobody's buying jelly beans.
Who's doing the counting anyway?

His mind was set, long before.
He'll sell it anyway he can
and call the bluff:

Trust me, there's no other way,
there's nothing to fear.
We must return to yesteryear.
Most won't feel anything
and beat the odds quite easily.
Some will get a little fever,
a headache and some flu.
But less than two percent will die.
Maybe less than one percent.
A lot less than one percent.
I heard maybe a tenth of a percent.
Mostly old people.
Blacks. People with pre-conditions.
Losers.

April 13, 2020 Week 6

Trumpius: Ways to Stay Safe From the Virus

Drink 1 part Lysol, 2 parts Mountain Dew, 2 glasses a day.

Wear MAGA hats, the virus does not like the color red.

Wash face with ammonia. I just know these things.

Keep social distance from anyone with an accent.

Keep social distance from suspected democrat persons.

Mix small amounts of isopropyl alcohol with your beer.
and drink American beer like Budweiser. *

Ultraviolet light: Only use thin plastic light sources to insert in anus.

Play golf. There's no virus on a golf course.

People die from food poisoning. You don't see us closing down the food industry. Eat fried chicken.

Take baths in windshield washing fluid.

Keep ovens on 450 all night, Sweep up dead virus in the morning.

If the virus kills a family member, blame the Dems.

April 20, 2020 Week 7

trump change

what little is left in the pocket
a few coins for a forbidden fountain
with scanty sentimental value
way back when   we knew
everything would get fucked up
we all knew that   o let it be known we knew
and here we are   afraid to open the front door
afraid to imagine the future

whatever ungodly revenge the earth takes on us
there are loses we must accept
but for whatever reasons in or out of his control
bottom line   i'm living like a fucking mole
in house arrest for nothing i've done
at war with a zombie virus and getting poor
an ample finish to these years
    the country is on lockdown
    the markets fall apart
    the bread lines grow
    the treasury is bankrupt
    the government is corrupt
    half the country hates the other
    thousands die each day
    in an unprecedented lack of empathy

he did good   kept his word   *I alone can fix this*
everything from top to bottom is fucked up

the public wishing wells are closed
until further notice.

April/May, 2020 Week 8

Morning Council at the Trumpius Desk

"Mr. President let me put it this way…
We have 350 million in the account.
Every year we have a little loss, but we have gain.
This is birth. More people are born than die."

Gotcha

"We earn a steady 60% a year increase birth/death ratio.
Our problem with the China Virus is right here,
see, where it fits on the chart in front of you.
This shows how many people die each year, and from what.
As this simple chart shows…
now, if we look at the chart…
Ahem, sir, the chart…

the virus will kill about as many as these:
accidents, lung diseases, and stroke,
if you can follow the pointer, sir."

Who would have known that!

"But see here: heart disease, cancer, Alzheimer's.
Look at those numbers, those are the really big numbers!".

We might play that up.
It's not like cancer or anything…

"Sir, you ARE a stable genius!"

May, 2020 Week 9

Trumpius is Mad Againe

April was too cruel   he's up to fifty tweets
Before breakfast   he's a tweet machine
Sweet revenge is all that he can think

Like a medieval king he sets the stage
Pounds the desk with madness and rage
He's fed up with the phony plague

Inflated statistics   the testing obscene
The White House now in quarantine
He takes aim at his enemies

He's the brand of his own disease
An addiction to a sweet nicotine
For the morally dead and morbidly obese

Sitting by their old Victrolas
With cellphones on their lap
Petting them like purring cats

While soothsayers interpret the signs
Conspiracy   deceit   deep state crimes
Inventing truth between the lines

If he could just cut out their tongues
The scientists   the press   the scum
Forget the wacko virus   it's over and done

Why then Ile fit you. Trumpius is mad againe.
Delirious Disorientated Demented
Bullshit bullshit bullshit

May 16, 2020 Week 10

Notes: The year of COVID

Panic Fear Armageddon, March 2020: Week 1
Corona virus is poorly understood, and the whole world starts to shut down, staying at home, watching TV. All institutions are closed. Trump tests negative for the virus. America fears to be as Europe, with spreading death and lack of hospital responses. Trumpius calls the news media "scum".

Daily Briefing Rage, March 2020: Week 2
Masks are first suggested, confusion about the virus continues as Americns start to die, and Europe suffers. Trumpius gives daily briefings to the public.

Essay: Plague in the Time of Marcus Aurelius, and Trumpius: Maximus By Marcus Eumolpus, Historian, April, 2020: Week 4
Marcus Aurelius is often falsely blamed for the persecution of the early Christians. Regional governors did from time to time enforce hardships, accusing the new religion for the pandemic, which Aurelius did not approve of. But he did not interfere, as were the rights of the states. Aurelius had a soft spot for the new god and wished to add it to the other deities. It seems once his troops won a battle because of a rainstorm, which allowed an advance to go unnoticed. The storm was said to have been prayed for by the followers of Jesus. Such beliefs in magic and the gods were commonly accepted in that time.

References:

"The Plague Under Marcus Aurelius and the Decline and Fall of the Roman Empire" by J. Rufus Fears, PhD, University of Oklahoma. © 2004 Elsevier Inc.

Quote by Zhou Enlai as told by a teammate at the local softball pickup game who went with Nixon in 1972 to China and attended the state dinner.

Trumpius Suggests Ways to Stay Safe From the Virus, April 20, 2020: Week 7

*FOX NEWS FACT CHECK: Budweiser Beer is owned and operated by a Belgian Company

Morning Council at the Trumpius Desk, May 9, 2020: Week 9

U.S. deaths from COVID reaches 90,000 in less than 3months, projected 160,000 fatalities by year's end.

Note: actual deaths by year's end was approximately 375,000

Trumpius is Mad Againe, May 16, 2020: Week 10

With acknowledgement to T.S. Eliot, *il miglior fabbro.*

Part Four: BLM, Pre-election Jitters

A Father at the Acquittal of a Cop Killing

The stage and cameras set up by my door,
My knees are shaking, my gut is numb.
A white politician taps my shoulder
And whispers in my ear, "this is your moment,
History calls ordinary men to be extraordinary.
You will be seen in the homes of America.
Make your son proud, let goodness guide you,
As he now rests quietly among the angels.
Be a hero for unity, and call for calm-
Be a man of peace like your Martin Luther King."

And so I stand before the multitude, my son's picture
On posters, chanting his name, as speakers
Say their litanies of thoughts and prayers.
Cellphones are held high, flowers cover my lawn,
The satellite dishes point to the cloudless heaven
As the police construct barriers around me.
Suddenly I see my son the day he understood the world;
He appears to me, as he was alive, but strangely older:
"Dad, do as you raised me, say what's in your heart."

"America, my black brothers and sisters,
A white cop has killed my son. My son. My son.
He killed my son because our lives are cheap to him.
I want the heart of his son, here, ripped out of his chest,
That is the only fitting revenge. Then will this murderer know
What he has done. What he has done.
What's that I hear? It's not our way?
It's not what I'm supposed to say?
We are civilized, believers in god and law,
We don't call an eye for an eye, no, not we.
Here we preach forgiveness. Forgiveness.
Follow that white Jesus you infected us with.

But let there be no calm. O, don't loot. O, don't shoot.
They just love to call it 'the natives are restless'.
They now brand our martyr- Martin Luther Coon.
What has changed since the day he crossed that bridge?
What does it mean to be calm and never hug my son again?

So let there be no calm. For I shall cry
Till the rage is buried with me in the grave.
What man, black or white, could love a country
Where a bad cop kills his son, and goes free?"

June, 2020

Sunday in June: Trumpius Trailing

There'll be silences. There'll be death of disbelief.
We have known the taste of sea sickness for years,
Our lives disrupted with political passions.

In twilight the birds return.
We'll hear the carnival drums in the distance
Announcing dancing down the avenue.
There'll be shouting from the rooftops and balconies,
Like never heard before, sighs of relief,
From a tedious illness of stomach pain.

Trumpius broods, a redemption at hand!
All polls agree: He will lose, he will lose!

> (O my anxious foolish self, tis' merely June,
> There's months to go before it's through.
> What war shall be declared; what junta assumed?
> The nightmare takes a pause…
>
> But, this poem felt good to do).

June, 2020

100 Days to the Election

A lyric with music

O sick America
Standing on hot coals till November
The great experiment's final quest
To break the fever or expire
To Trumpius and his reign of fire

O sick America
On a ventilator in the ICU
We listen to your heartbeat
Your blood spinning in a centrifuge
To purify demons of elections past

O sick America
Our dream spangled daughter
Freedom is frail before our eyes
No parent can bare to lose a child
You must   you must survive
You must   you must survive

July 20, 2020

Comorbidities

the simultaneous presence of two chronic diseases or conditions in a patient

Repeat: Person Man Woman Camera TV
Try: Baboon Female Appetite Airplane Customs
Again: Detergent Football Crime Buddha Dance
Now: Ekphrastic Spinozaa Antelope Purple Envy

Results: Patient Trumpius
Patient suffers from "Bipolar Synesthesia"
A condition common in alpha males.

His niece, a therapist, says,
As a boy he would
Pin the tail on the elephant
Not the donkey.

Math skills:
Advanced Dyscalculia.
There is no cure.

Signs of acute Talkiswalkism.
Irascible with hysterical rages.

Recommendation:
To the estates on the Ile of Saint Helena
Complete with golden urinal
And state of the art putting green.
Suggest hydroxychloroquine to sleep.

August, 2020

Cable News 2020

Everyone's in on the debate, it's sprinkled on your cornflakes. Start the day with the morning crew; coffee, Tums and cable news.

Fox News

The natives on the loose
With painted faces the Dems the Dems
Unholy perverts and pinko commies
They them the Dems the Dems
(Oh, that "how'd I get here" pile of shit
When Tucker Carlson does his bit!)
It's those damn Jews, the fake news Jews,
They'll cheat the souls off your shoes.
Hide the ammo. Hide the guns.
They'll take away your Christmas fun.
Laura Ingram's smirky face.
We have negroes in the base!
Who's a racist? Just says here,
Mexicans should drink Mexican beers.
Things should remain that way,
The USA's one big Conspira-Say:
Socialism, Atheism, FBI,
Deep State, alien flu, CIA,
Faggot politics and immigrant stew.

MSNBC

Almost four years of it,
The chatter of revulsion.
It comes off philosophical
But it's clear as a barking dog:
Pity for stupidity has turned to hate;
We despise them, loathe them,
Demonize them. Mock them.

Tease them. They disgust us.
Dumb-fucking-village-idiots.
Old-white-trash-racist-bastards.
They have two assholes, two brains,
One of which is senile or insane,
And the other one neanderthal,
Sucking up the moron's tweets
Like he's the High Holy Ghost himself
Whose shit doesn't stink.

***

The storms will settle down, like times before,
After the banging of shoe heels on the doors,
When cable news rules our lives no more-
We'll fill the day with daily chores,
Classical music, weather and sports.

The headlines will simply disappear
Like COVID was supposed to do.

Let us wear masks from ear to ear,
Muttering to ourselves, "enough of news".
Till then we growl our snarls and grunts
Without a truce to be lost or won.

August, 2020

The Market is Up

"The market is up BIG today"
Trumpius Tweet 9/17/20

Seas have fever   lightening has wings
A few hundred thousand more
Shall cough themselves to death
All's red in day and black at night
Thank god the stock market is alright

Whales are butchered   elephants rot
Milk is sour   bees diseased
Rains are packed with soot and grime
Steeples collapse   church bells crack
401k's are still on track

Plastic coats the ocean floor
Redwoods in a wall aflame
Steeples topple   church bells crack
Malls are filled with urine smell
At least the market's doing well

We little people and our precious gains
We suffer so terribly   again and again
Because the market crashes in the end.

September, 2020

10/3/20: Page From Diary

Saturday 11:00. Try to write a rhyme poem.
Trumpius in hospital with COVID.
Call Bruce, buy soy milk creamer.

We had hoped the debate would be the stage
That somehow the animal would stay in his cage.
We were betrayed again, Trumpius rattled and raged,
Indecency was on trial and civility upstaged.
For days we walked in silence, dazed and amazed,
And now news he has COVID. For what we had prayed.

Really? Now what?
Do I wish him dead? Have I taken some Hippocratic oath, that good men of poetry defend the sick? Do I feel cheated? He might die and I would have to watch the long parade of chubby women, the ministers praising his soul from the golf course, the carnival of armed motor gangs with their Mad Max dreams and hard core metal rock and roll, to hear the hopes and prayers by all who have named him America's porta potty, and hear the pundits sigh…
Do I really wish him dead?

It could it be worse if he survives, to tell the world, "It's what I said, no big deal, a bad cold, I never was in fear", with a quarter million dead with at least the same to come…his recovery to rally the faithful; he's truly a god, the savior of tribal brains, and voted in again…or worse, to lose and refuse to leave office as the nation ignites in in burning flames, goin' up in smoke. So what's the verdict? Thumbs up or down? An astrological premonition.

My wish: Trumpius stays ill as a rabid dog for months, resigns, leaves Walter Reade like Saddam Hussein, having found the inner peace of Allah before he was hanged. But no! Let the fake news and courts torture him for years, for the addicted among us who can't forego hate; he lives for revenge, as do we. Hate is a two way street. It will take time to heal. Look what I wrote way back then : "This will very likely not end well".
*** USE IN END OF BOOK**

Today I feel no hope for the days and weeks
I will not be healed. For whatever the verdict,
During the time I wrote this therapeutic rattle.
Forty more coughed themselves to the grave.
*** PUT INTO RHYME**

October 3, 2020

This Will Very Likely Not End Well

A third of the nation is in fantasylands
Of aliens and the zombie apocalypse.
In farmlands the fields are blooming
With signs for Trumpius and Pence.
Vague threats and fingers a pointin'
This will very likely not end well.

How did foolery became buffoonery,
That somehow, this IS reality?
How could one man carve up the state
So carefully with contempt and hate?
The bell in the steeple waits silently
This will very likely not end well.

The play is filled with subplots of greed,
Mad scene of a Shakespearean tragedy,
While the Great White Hope, the GOP,
No longer disguises their beliefs,
Courting votes from supremacy
This will very likely not end well.

Every minute another soul departs
As the COVID winter settles in.
The arrogance is evangelical,
But the arrow of truth has pierced the ankle-
A conspiracy theory says we're going to hell
This will very likely not end well.

November 2, 2020

Notes: BLM, Pre-election Jitters

A Father at the Acquittal of a Cop Killing, June, 2020
Shocking videos of police brutality and killings. Huge demonstrations for Black Lives Matter around the world. Trumpius calls them "terrorists".

Sunday in June: Trumpius Behind, June, 2020
Anticipation of voting Trumpius out of office begins, polls say he is losing. All remember, we cannot trust the polls!

Comorbidities, August, 2020
After a book by his niece published, with accusations of sociopathic behavior, Trumpius takes "Mental Health Test".
"Talkiswalkism: The Problem with Believing Everything You Say" Jeremy E. Sherman Ph.D., MPP
"Hydroxychloroquine" the absurd, unproven pharmaceutical treatment which Trumpius championed for COVID-19.

Part Five: The Election

Election Day

> "the good itself is not essence but it …transcends
> essence in dignity…" Plato, the Republic

All was to be forgotten.
All was to be redeemed.
All was to be forgiven.
Biden will transcend our essence
With the common dignity.
The forecast is for calm seas.

How the hell did we put up with it?
Four years; every morning to the news,
Every cup of coffee, every topic of the day,
The background chatter, a plague of lies
Metastasized to tumors of the mind.
Locked-down, tied-up in knots, afraid.

Tell me, how long are years? How they blur away!
It seems so long we waited for this day,
This moment, this brief held moment,
How we remember, while the wound remains,
How years passed with a rusted needle in our veins
    to fill with shame and disgust-
Trumpius and his shitty tweets…
The country's soul gauged-out like eyes
Blinded by this fucking liar. Lies! Lies! Lies!

Why this seething for revenge?
This aftermath of shell-shocked ruins?
Maybe tomorrow we'll start to heal,
Face a future bankrupt in despair.
Forget the whole affair. But not today.
Today the future gets declared.

November 3, 2020, afternoon

Election Eve: Two Countries

After Jose Marti

Two countries have I now: America and the GOP.
Or are they the same? The passport once revered,
With the arrogant ownership of hope-
What innocence of spirit, once a melting pot,
With a common cause to hold ground above the greed
  that occupies the ways of power. America
The compassionate, America of laws supreme,
Never the fate of kingdoms with kings
Crowned by coup d'états regimes. America!

How the sadness grows, families become as nations,
Torn apart. Who among us has not seen our roots
Which issued their complaints against the grain,
Lost to bygone days, so much has strayed, Irretrievable.

The morning call to prayer
Praises the destroyer god.
America the widow.

November 3, 2020, night

The Winkies

We sit on our couches before a flat TV
With a mask around our memories.
Four years have passed, the years resound
Disbelief from when the scourge began-
Four years since Trumpius took that escalator down,
His Cleopatra wife smirking by his side,
Cursing all the immigrants, our dignity on trial,
Selling *Make America Great Again.*

We wait for the final count; Biden leads.
But Trumpius screams, refuses defeats,
Sends his lawyers with stupid schemes
To demand new rulings from the jury.
As we spend hours tossing and turning-
The election map turns red to blue.
Courts will refuse to hear conniving-
¡Viva la Republica! Death to fake news!

The pundits plead for our compassion-
Let us forgive these kind and meager folk,
Our Winkies, the soup of despicables'.
They huddle in their church of guns and sin.
They will see it our way, let's take them in!

But those folks have red faces,
filled with bloody flares.
They hate me and all I stand for,
And they ain't goin' anywhere.

November 4, 2020

Hope Betrayed

Devastated, shocked, dismayed
The count runs through the day
Into the night of long delays
Trumpius tweets with usual rage.

The soul of the country on display
Racism, climate change, deadly plague,
Locked-down, tied in knots, afraid,
The election shows of what we're made-

Heartburn, nausea, anger, pain,
The years ahead, nothing to gain.
Biden winning, with hope betrayed
And dignity left to decay.

November 5, 2020

Saturday 11:50 AM EST

When I heard the shouts in the street,
The cars honking and bells ringing, I said,
Let there be loud music in my life again!
Beethoven, Mahler, Verdi? No, Boito,
From the opera Mephistopheles, the finale.

I found it on Youtube, watched several times over
blasting in my headphones like
sticking my head inside a trumpet,
So the sound went through me in electrical blasts
And my body buzzed with jubilation!

Sam Ramey the baritone, with orange hair,
O holy triumph of good over evil-
Such rage and arrogance against the cherubim
As the tenor hits a high note with the good book
in his hand to curse and burn the lies.
The kettle drums roll, the slide whistles chime,
All the sound 's a thunder of deafening conclusion,
The stage fills with roses from the balconies
And Trumpius is carried away like a demon
squirming in the flames.

And I too was released.

November 7, 2020

Dementia Moment

That film you saw once, and forgot you'd seen,
At the very end you realize "I know this scene!"

It all comes back; the episodes of this shocking age,
The story of the Trumpius years. Now our heritage:

The boarder wall, the Muslim ban, Charlottesville,
Paper towels in San Juan, separating children

Into cages without mothers, Hallmark Cards to overlords,
Orwellian propaganda tweets, impeached and deplored,

The porn star, the Russian probes, the conspirators in jail,
The racist trolls, ugly ties, demonizing mail,

Bar room imbecilities, science denied, truth decay,
Wind turbines cause cancer, all Dems are gay ...

It took a quarter million dead, his empty vial of tears,
The corpses fill the trucks as all had feared,

As the people rose to vote, stood hours in the rain,
In a pandemic, to cast the sin away.

I will not forget the scene! Fade out, his unkempt hair,
The soundtrack plays a twangy tune: *It wasn't fair.*

The worst rating ever on Rotten Tomatoes. So sad.
I want my money back.

November 9, 2020

Götterdämmerunging the USA

Saturday 10 AM: Morning Coffee

It's done. I'm done. We are over and done.
Counting days when we say *cheerio.*
What will be, O patria mia, what's gonna be?

Trumpius will fly back to his villa in disgrace.
The wife files for divorce, the pundits laugh,
The silliness of frauds and deceit come to pass
As Biden soothes a panicked press-
Trumpius said this, then he said that…
Relax. Joe is here to redeem the past.

Trumpius plays the spoiled and rotten brat,
In a tantrum he trashes the Oval Office.
Ripping the curtains and shattering decanters
Mumbling over and over again, *I was cheated big time.*
Nothing can ever change his mind, millions of votes
behind his back, cast by evil Democrats…

So we all ask, what will become of us now?
Where shall we find the soul of America?
The pandering goes on as long as he's alive-
The cult of the snake, the head of the tribe.

1 PM: Stroll Around the National Mall

This year the fall came like the spring,
Warm in yellowness, as it began.

Leaves flutter with a whispering warm
Filling the ground with bright forlorn.

No matter where in the capital town
Everyone is smiling behind the mask.

4 PM: Writer's Desk

Here you must end this tale.
How long could it go on?
It's all in denouement, redundant,
Chatterchatterchatter in the air waves.
The curtain closed, the crowd is booing-
The empire survives by a horse's nose.

There is no more to take from it.
Here it ends, Trumpius is out of my life,
I feign I will go mad if I do not act so!
I'm serious now, no more poetry voice,
I mean it, damn it, I'm getting Trumpius out
Out of my brain, my fantasies, my dreams,
 I'm gonna knock that Trumpius
 Outta my head, gonna knockknockknock

This is the end, the blood fever,
The Vulcan Ritual of Tal Dreck,
Eumolpus, too, is mad againe-
Everybody chanting *hit the road Jack,*
Don't come back no more no more no more.
Let's make it the National Anthem!
Trumpius, hit the road, and don't come back.

November 10, 2020

Postscript: November 16, 2020

So here I am at last! I made it alive! Four years ago, I took to the task of addressing current events by writing poems. It evolved as a project to write one each month. They are centered around Trumpius, with some exceptions; the evil and stupidity was too epic! In these last months, during COVID-19 quarantine and with ridiculous briefings, the election and all that lead up to it, I had little else on my mind and added poems almost daily. Even as I write this emotions are high, due to the White House refusal to accept the election, as we were warned. (Are we so different than Rome, really?) Trumpius fires some hated generals, and runs helter-skelter as his party stands by, waiting for marching orders. But every hour the roller-coaster is slowing down. Every day is lighter. The world leaders have sent their new envoys. Even the odds makers in Las Vegas know it's over. They are always right. *It's all over but the shoutin'*. Time to move on to other poems. Perhaps about death, or spring, or the boys of summer in their ruin…

The Trumpius years will be the subject of many historical books, novels, maybe an opera or two, perhaps some poetry. Thank the gods just barely enough of our citizens wanted to be finished with this chapter of our history and voted. Trumpius will, no doubt, remain in the background, irritating a wounded America until the end. It will take years digging out of this ditch. He's actually considering running again in 2024. That would be most unlikely. Soon he will be like COVID. A bad dream. A Loser.

Time will tell if I achieved my goal, that far in the future when Trumpius and I are gone, that these attempts will give a glimpse of this time through poetry. Though very tempting, I did very few revisions, trying to be true to the moment. Such was my intent all along in this "historical document", on the edge of my seat for four years. Some of the anticipated events never happened, like a big war, but "normalcy" was subjected to daily attack and every tradition of dignity and law was challenged.

Can political poetry avoid being propagandistic or preachy? As I re-read the poems now as a whole, of course many of the poems were reduced to rants, the insult of Trumpism being so polarizing. Here is biblio-therapy at work. There is an inevitable redundancy in themes. Changing poetic forms and devices does not change that, but each carries its own weight. The events were both real and metaphorical.

I am a bit amused that when I wrote "Author's Note to Self", in 2017, " this will very likely not end well." One thing for sure, this was, and is, a surreal time to live. Are these times any crazier than those with Hitler, Stalin, Philip the Cruel or whoever?

It appears Biden does have a chance to be a great historical figure who unites the country with grace. The story continues, but any odes to be found about Trumpius will fall flat, as his reign of outrageous buffoonery. But there is hope. Joe Biden quotes from Seamus Heany.

***

If we see the Civil War as Strike One, we have just dodged Strike Two. Strike Three, we may be out. For example, the delcine of the Dutch empire in the 17th century. In the book "Embarrassments of Riches", Daniel Boorstin shows how all the wealth went to the top, and corruption ruled, with a declining middle class. They were doomed. Are we too?

There is hope the Hegelian cuckoo clock will swing back towards progress, maybe we won't return to the reactionaries for a while. Maybe we'll have a decade like the Roaring Twenties, which followed the Spanish Flu. Yes, bring back the jitterbug for a while.

Once I heard Gabriel Garcia Márquez discussing South America's politics of juntas and strong men, and the USA. He considered how the Magna Carter, in 1215, established in England a semblance of law and democratic principles. It takes generations to make it normal for townspeople to expect equality and the rights of the individual. That ancient document passed to the young America, and instilled the belief and faith that no one is above the law. That's why we cherish the most, our orderly government. It may take a little longer in South America, and most of the world, to catch up. Democracy must be instilled in the blood of the people. That was the gift from Greece to Rome to England, to today. More Americans voted in the election of 2020 than ever before. This may be the one good thing to come out of this whole affair, as the public woke up to the fact that politics do matter if we seek to save our democracy. Maybe globalization will make the whole world *woke*.

And Mr. Fukuyama has become a democrat.

November 16, 2020

Notes: The Election

The Winkies, November 4, 2020

In the Wizard of Oz, the Winkies were a kindly people. They were frightened by the Wicked Witch of the West, and became her protectors and police force. In the film, they had green painted faces. When the Witch melted away, the people rejoiced and gave Dorothy the broom to present to the Wizard and returned to their former good will. In the book, Winkies were great craftsmen.

Sat 11:50 AM EST, November 6, 2020

One can also refer to any good recording of the finale of Boito's Mephistopheles. But this one is noteworthy. Play at full blast! https://bit.ly/3tCPujT

Postscript:, November 16, 2020

The end of an era. Well, not quite…the wake-up call was traumatic, and the shock will be felt for generations to come.

Part Six: The Aftermath

Post Postscript

January 8, 2021 4 AM

And I thought it was all over but the shouting.
We all did, the shouting was over, a lifetime ago.

What more to be said? What new can be said of it?
The post-election trauma of Trumpius-
The battle was over, now the burning of the dead.

Who can sleep? A writer writes.
It was like having food poisoning,
When you can hold it back no longer.

1PM Saturday, Live From D.C.

At first I was reminded. Way back I stormed into the dean's office with the Students for a Democratic Society demanding liberty, equality, fraternity, to change the world by chanting slogans. Not this mob. They came for a prized selfie to show the grandkids; *Burning my voting card in Washington D.C.* Hang it in the family room.

America, I'm drowning in the pathetic, another shot to a body riddled with bullets of bullshit. O sad, sad country. What have you allowed to pass? It was not *just* a mob. It was the face of heartland America. Truly are we a Roman Circus. What charisma do the Populusque Trumpius see? Is there no potion to cleanse this vulgarity? No, this was not an unruly student riot. Back then I only had the blind optimism of a pampered youth. But we were merely against an unjust war, not trying to overthrow our democracy and change our republic to a dictatorship.

We see the footage over and over, in disbelief: history IS disbelief. Today the Goths or the Huns are not from northern forests, not from the lands without roads where bands of savages roam. They are among us. They are the pessimism of senility. America is getting old.

Why can't things be as they were? There are no repeat performances. I'm drowning in the pathetic. They came to defile the sacred chambers of the state and when they got to the pulpit they took their selfies. There was nothing else for them to do.

Revolutionaries for the fascist state, chanting slogans to *Stop the Steal.* The world too, was watching the latest episode of American Exceptionalism. A mob of drunk soccer fans looking for a fight.

January 9, 2021

Fox News Defines Socialism

"I explained to my children that socialism is when the government comes to your house to take your backpacks"
Commentator, Fox News

Socialism is hermaphrodites in the public stalls.
Socialism is hearing gangsta raps songs.

Poets are socialists, yoga teachers too.
Socialists hate guns and everything we do.

Socialists are atheists, robot makers, climate changers.
Socialism is Medicare care for all them strangers.

Socialists are kosher, also known as Jews.
Socialists, communists, wear the same hat too!

The problem is, see, they're brainwashed or gay
And only hear what other socialists say!

January 15, 2021

Letter to the Editor: Convict!

I

The old guard, Plato and Socrates, invented our democracy
And warned that every citizenry will have a mob mentality.
Democracy will fail if a plebe can be the president-
Leads to anarchy, autocracy, and fall to common thievery:
The state must breed the best, choose among their creed
To govern all with dignity, serve the people and their needs-
This was Plato's vision for revision of humanity.
A possibility from 300 BC, a utopian society.
But this will never come to be; it's far beyond reality.

The founders knew the Greeks, and feared the tragic fault
Of men, and failed to give the wives the right to vote,
Or dared to let a colored man take the highest post-
This would wait for centuries to make its way,
But quelled the mob to save the people from themselves
And give power to the people's vote,
To end the greed of bloody thrones.
We thought we had a common decency.
We were indeed naïve, that citizens had civility:
Drowning in conspiracies, seeing not believing
What is right before them on the TV screen;
Liberty's not free from its excesses to be free-
The founders, before technology, before electricity
Sent their urgent messages attached to pigeon's wings.
Now is a time of siege that no one thought we'd see.
We cannot find unity and ignore the new confederacy.
A confederacy of lies, an infection, a fascist insurrection,
Sirens blasting false alarms for a phony resolution.
We are stunned to see our sacred nation go to revolution.

II

He's been twice impeached for his odious tweets.
He's the at the pulpit of this historical bleep.
We speak of reparations going on for generations
Awaiting resurrections, for we must change directions,

And nothing will until the monster's caged
And the filthy mouth shuffled off the stage.
Our hope to show the world, America's still wise,
Not dumb-ass stupid as the ancients prophesized.
So we must convict, to heal, the wound is deep
Not let the generations remember us as sheep.

January 18, 2021

Inauguration Day

Trumpius No More

America was sucking oxygen as the COVID kills
You were selling pardons at the window sill.

Next to Nefertiti, how your neck and shoulders slump.
Walk the plank to air-force one and be gone, Citizen Trump!

Foiled again! I can hear in your behemoth rage
Offering us a fingered salute enroute to an alligator cage.

Ahead are years of satire, America's buffoon,
Your name scratched from the obelisks, in ruins.

Never to be Maximus: a mere name with no suits,
The folly of a pussy grabber, a mafioso, a brute.

You had your Waterloo. Tweet no more, fly away.
Exiled to swamps until called before the jury

For every time you jaywalked or extorted to a judge,
For every conniving lie so uncouth and outrageous!

Humpty Trumpy fell from his wall, Humpty Trumpty
Fell bigly . Thy heart is cruel, thy words, empty.

Now splattered and spiting like a snake
Sounding no different asleep than awake,

And all the Proud Boys, and all Hannity's men,
Can't put you back together again.

Joe. Just Joe. Joe.

It is written all over him: Joe.
Lovely, soft spoken eyes, the one who knows pain-
Fearless Joe. Tea with honey Joe.
Some hate Joe because they fear he speaks the truth.

That will change. It will take years. Joe waits.
Joe knows. He has suffered
To know the grace of patience.

Unlike us, with our faces clinched like fists,
There is scant hatred in his eyes.
Maybe it is that which is common to the healers:
Gandhi, Mandela, or Martin Luther King-
A fragile charm from the depth of sadness,
A thing that comes from the gut to deliver tears
On a voyage to find goodness in us, the common people.
From all the different regions, classes, religions, affiliations;
Because he believes, we can believe.
This is the great American experiment.

Joe, keep singing that over and over for years.
We are a nation of consumers, we are what we eat.
Your words are the recipe we need.
This is the Thanksgiving that is America,
Our tables full with an abundance of hope,
Feeling a wind of scented candles.
Every man and woman is Joe.
President Joe!

January 20, 2021

The Big Lie or A Final Rant

Three months later...

It doth appear the wolf hath escaped the gallows againe.
He now rests like the behemoth in a black sea,
As his agents endorse *The Big Lie,*
Sucking every dollar from the gullible tribe.
Trumpius Maximus- history will not be kind!
On your grave will be inscribed the famous plea;
Nobody was treated so badly as me!
Yet the tale continues, the wolf doth gather the troops,
For one last Waterloo! He plans his resurrection,
And shall run again in Twenty-Four! He shall not fade,
Another Fidel, another Franco. Insurrection is the tide.
Apocalyptic times ahead, filled with dread.

***

The ancients prayed to snakes and golden cows.
How is it we are no better? From the first day
Populusque Trumpius, tattooed in stupidity,
Without shame or care, proclaimed
It was the greatest inauguration ever!
Welcome the age of "alternative facts".
Alternative fucking facts! Well,
Fuck you, Kellyanne! Fuck you!
And you Bill Barr, and you Vomit Mouth,
And you vile and villainous Nunes
And Jarad and your fucking squeaky voice,
And Ms. *i don't really care do u*?
And Giuliani, who will die in disgrace,
And Bitch McConnell, and the millions
In the holy base of the GOP.
It's just a situation comedy,
An infection, an Embarrassment of Riches,
America the Cold, the Crude, America the Sterile.
Ultra! Basta! Enough!! Amen!!!

***

My friend, maker of verses, Petronius Arbiter-
I too cannot bear our Nero's insidious voice,
I can listen no more to the poisoned irony!
The gnawing bestiality he smells of,
A horror show of a wretched bourgeoisie.
He has sold the soul of the patria
To be worshipped in the trailer parks,
Where the dispossessed agree en masse-
Blame the shamers who cancel Christmas!

The Big Lie! Socrates and truth again on trial!
We who dream democracy- rant on!
Has there ever been a POTUS more despised?
When was there such scum, and folly of deceit?
A puss filled boil on the face of the nation.
Rant again we must hiss and cuss and cry
And foam at the mouth and holler our heads off
Should the pig emerge from his sty
While the hemlock remains in the vial.

These are days of dim, they are, days of dim.
The Big Lie thrives in a carnival of fear.
Nothing is forgotten, and nothing redeemed.
A darkness descends on the American dream.
There is no greater sadness: nothing is real.

April 20, 2021

Notes: The Aftermath

1PM Saturday, Live from D.C., January 9, 2021
On January 6th, Trumpius incites a crowd of thousands of his followers, resulting in the violent storming the Capitol. Their purpose was to disrupt the Congress from confirming the results of the Electoral Votes, which had elected Joe Biden. Innocent people died, chaos reigned. After many hours the National Guard was called in. Later in the night, Congress returned to their chambers and confirmed Biden, as the 46th President of the United States.

Letter to the Editor: Convict!, January 18, 2020
Trumpius was impeached for the second time by the House of Representatives, awaits the Senate vote. 25,000 National Guardsman are brought to the Capitol for the inauguration.

The Big Lie or A Final Rant, April, 20, 2021
75% of Republicans embrace "The Big Lie", that the election was somehow fixed or altered by a "Deep State" conspiracy and that Trumpius was the winner. He continues to be the head of greatest attack on reality and truth in modern times. It is simply unimaginable to try to reason with the followers of endlessly stupid conspiracies. Democracy shall be on trial for years to come.

May his image be ousted to the public toilets…
Eumolpus: The Meditations, II:14, AD 2021

Finis

About the Author

Mark Fishbein was born in Brooklyn, NY. After graduating from CCNY in 1971 with a BA in English Literature, he attended the Sorbonne in Paris and studied French Literature for two years. Upon returning to the US, he became an innovator in the emerging screen printing and t-shirt dyeing industry, while raising his family in New York City. He always kept "a book of poetry in his pocket".

After leaving the industry, Mark dedicated his time to his first love, poetry. He has written six books of poetry, most recently, *Reflections in the Time of Trumpius Maximus* (2021), *Stances* (2018) and an ekphrastic book, *Poems Hanging on a Wall* (2020). He has translated a collection by the French poet Paul Eluard. His poems have appeared in a variety of magazines and journals including*The Hill Rag* and *American Atheist Magazine.*

Online, Mark is a contributor and board member of PGN-Poetry Global Network. He is host to two writer's workshops, and a unique Zoom event; Planet Poetry 28, a monthly Virtual Poetry Journal introducing poets from around the world. Often Mark combines his live readings with his eclectic classical guitar style of music.

You can sign up for author updates and information about Mark's poetry workshops at **www.poetwithguitar.com**

About Atmosphere Press

Atmosphere Press is an independent, full-service publisher for excellent books in all genres and for all audiences. Learn more about what we do at atmospherepress.com.

We encourage you to check out some of Atmosphere's latest releases, which are available at Amazon.com and via order from your local bookstore:

The Unsolvable Intrigue, poetry by D.C. Stoy
Love, Air, poetry by Lawdenmarc Decamora
To Let Myself Go, poetry by Kimberly Olivera Lainez
less on that later, poetry by Madeline Farber
The Last Hello: 99 Odes to the Body, poetry by Joe Numbers
Granddaughter of Dust, poetry by Laura Williams
Nest of Stars, poetry by Nicole Verrone
Damaged, poetry by Crystal Wells
I Would Tell You a Secret, poetry by Hayden Dansky
Aegis of Waves, poetry by Elder Gideon
Footnotes for a New Universe, by Richard A. Jones
Streetscapes, poetry by Martin Jon Porter
Feast, poetry by Alexandra Antonopoulos
River, Run! poetry by Caitlin Jackson
Poems for the Asylum, poetry by Daniel J. Lutz
Licorice, poetry by Liz Bruno
Etching the Ghost, poetry by Cathleen Cohen
Spindrift, poetry by Laurence W. Thomas

CPSIA information can be obtained
at www.ICGtesting.com
Printed in the USA
LVHW020321031121
702257LV00018B/1450

9 781639 881390